CROSS STITCH ON THE MOVE

Jane Greenoff

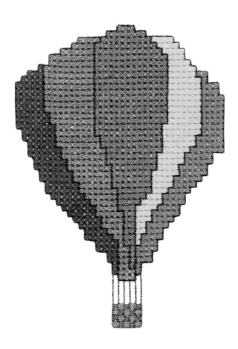

d&C

David & Charles

To my children, James Eric and Louise Estelle with love always

A DAVID & CHARLES BOOK

Copyright Text and designs © Jane Greenoff 1993
Copyright Photography © Simon Apps 1993
except photograph on pp16–17 © David & Charles 1993
Cover design stitched by Vera Greenoff

First published 1993

A catalogue record for this book is available from the British Library.

ISBN 0 7153 0070 9

Typeset by ABM Typographics L.d Hull
and printed in Italy by OFSA SpA
for David & Charles
Brunel House Newton Abbot Devon

contents

how to stitch

Counted cross stitch is one of the easiest types of embroidery.

All the designs are made up of squares which you reproduce on your fabric as cross stitches. In the next section [page 6] you will see how to read a chart.

YOU WILL NEED

To work a design from this book you will need threads, Aida fabric 11 blocks to 2.5cm [1 inch] and a blunt tapestry needle, size 24 or 22.

Some stitchers like to use a hoop or frame when they are working cross stitch. It is not essential for this type of work.

All the designs in the book were worked without a frame.

THE THREADS

All the stitched designs in this book have been worked in stranded cottons (floss). Each length of thread is made up of six strands of cotton (floss) and you usually divide each length before you start sewing.

All the cross stitch in this book is stitched using three strands of stranded cotton (floss).

It is a good idea to 'organise' your threads. At the bottom of the picture opposite you can see what I mean. The threads are cut into manageable lengths [50cm or 20 inches] and looped on to a piece of punched card like the one illustrated. This helps to stop tangles and knots.

THE FABRIC

All the designs in this book are stitched on Aida fabric. It is made of cotton and is specially woven for cross stitch. It looks as if it is made up of squares, which makes the counting much easier.

All the designs in the book are stitched from the centre of the fabric, which means you actually get the design in the middle. This is very important when you are ready to frame the finished piece.

The material used for cross stitch does tend to fray around the edges, so it is a good idea to neaten the edge in some way. Either fold over and stitch a narrow hem or oversew the edge loosely. This stitching can be pulled out when the work is finished.

HOW TO START

Divide the length of cotton (floss) and thread your needle with three strands.

Look at picture A opposite. Bring the needle up at point 1.

Leave a short end on the wrong side [see picture E].

Cross the square and go down through point 2.

Come up again at point 3.

Cross the square and go down through point 4. Note the position of the needle.

This half cross stitch can be repeated as in picture B, which shows how to complete the cross stitch. As you work each cross stitch on the material, it matches one square on the chart.

FINISHING OFF

To prevent the loose ends from undoing themselves, you will need to tie them off as you go. It is better not to use knots as they cause lumps and bumps that show on the front when the work is finished.

After working a few stitches, turn the work over to the wrong side and catch in the thread left at the start [see picture F].

When you have finished one colour, tie off the ends in the same way [see picture G].

Picture C shows that the top stitch should face the same way whether you are working up and down or from left to right.

Picture D illustrates how to add the backstitch outline around blocks of colour.

Picture H shows how to find the centre of the fabric and position the first stitch in the right place. Fold the fabric in half and then in half again. Press it lightly and work a line of tacking (basting) stitches along the folds. This will mark the position of the first-central-stitch. When you have finished cross stitching, remove these threads carefully.

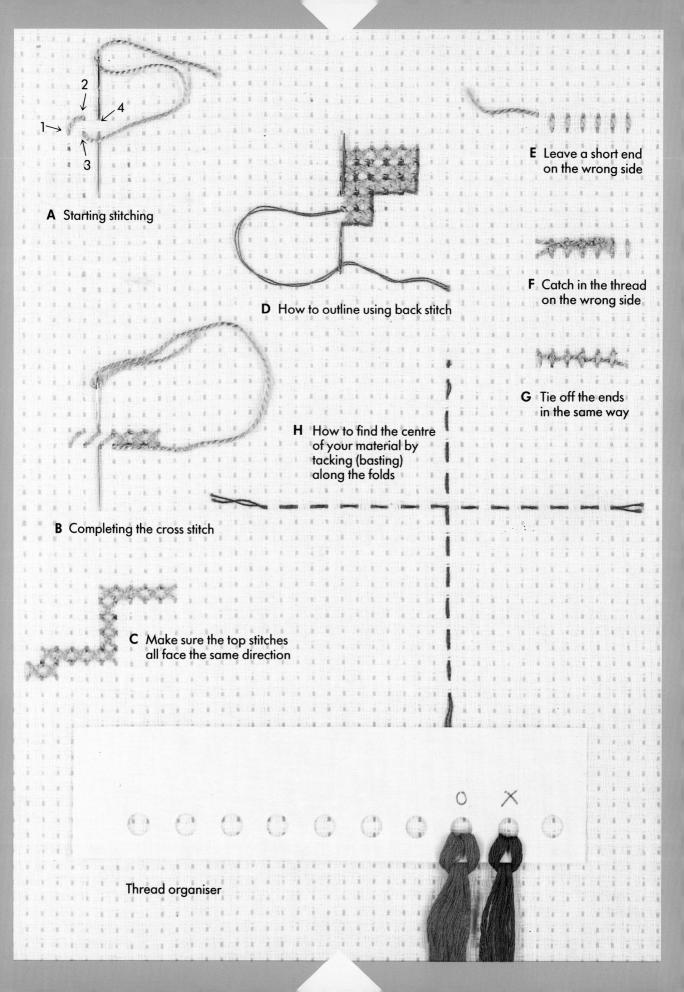

A Starting stitching

D How to outline using back stitch

E Leave a short end on the wrong side

F Catch in the thread on the wrong side

G Tie off the ends in the same way

H How to find the centre of your material by tacking (basting) along the folds

B Completing the cross stitch

C Make sure the top stitches all face the same direction

Thread organiser

how to read a chart

● On the page opposite you will see a large coloured chart of the hot-air balloon.

● This design is illustrated in the colour photograph on page 9. Full stitching instructions are on page 8.

● The hot-air balloon chart is drawn in felt-tip pens on squared paper.

● Each square on the paper represents one square on your fabric. As we discovered in the picture on page 5, the Aida fabric used for all the stitching in this series of books is also made up of squares.

● All the charts in the book are drawn in the same way. Each one has a list of the colours used next to the symbol in the key. The hot-air balloon is made up of red, blue, green, yellow, orange, chestnut, honey and dark blue outline.

● Each chart has the central square marked.

You can see that the first stitch on the hot-air balloon is green. As with each project, the instructions for the hot-air balloon show you where to start and in which direction to stitch. You will soon get the idea.

● All the symbols are worked in cross stitch in the colour listed in the key. You can use any colour or brand of thread you like, but if you want to copy the design in the colour photograph exactly, you will need DMC stranded cotton (floss). The shade numbers are included in each project.

● The solid outlines around the stitching are worked in back stitch when the cross stitch has been completed [see pages 4 and 5]. You can see that the outline of the hot-air balloon is stitched in dark blue.

notes for parents and teachers

The pleasure adults find in all forms of needlework is often denied children today for all sorts of reasons. At school the needs of the national curriculum have left little or no time for children to experiment with embroidery. It is also a fact that many young parents were not taught needlework and are learning themselves!

Counted cross stitch is one of the simplest, least expensive and most rewarding types of needlecraft and is suitable for all ages and both sexes!

My own experience of teaching children under ten has been a revelation. The children concerned were volunteers after school hours and were mostly boys. After learning the basic stitch and how to read a chart, the entire group was designing and stitching in less than two weeks.

The most successful children were those whose first project was small and quickly completed. They were therefore eager to experiment.

I even know of one school who used counted cross stitch as a maths project. Surface areas were calculated, ratio and proportion were considered and percentages were studied.

HOW TO HELP

1   Choose small projects with large blocks of colour.
2   Select fabric that can be seen clearly and handled easily.
    Aida cloth is available in 8, 11, 14, 16 and 18 blocks to 2.5cm [1 inch].
3   Use blunt tapestry needles with large eyes in size 24 or 22.
4   Be prepared to thread and re-thread needles to start with. You may find it helpful to have a number of threaded needles ready for use!
5   Encourage the stitcher as much as possible, helping over any difficult bits. It may lead to hours of peace and quiet later when he or she is hooked!

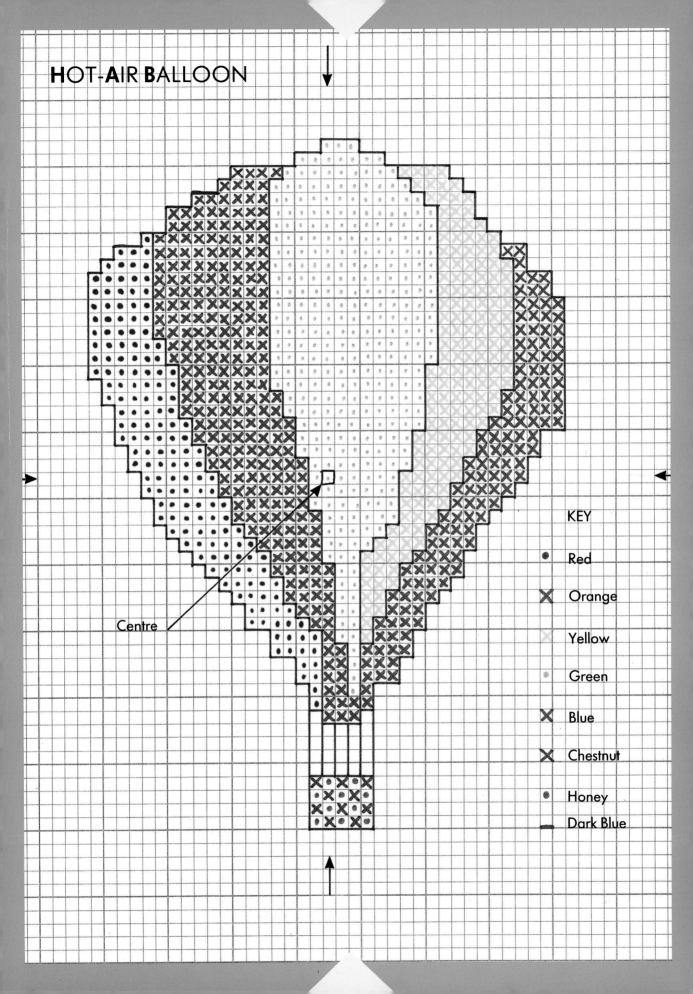

HOT-AIR BALLOON

Centre

KEY

● Red

✕ Orange

✕ Yellow

● Green

✕ Blue

✕ Chestnut

● Honey

— Dark Blue

HOT-AIR BALLOON

CHART KEY

COLOUR	DMC	ANCHOR
Red	349	046
Blue	340	0118
Green	562	0216
Yellow	743	0298
Orange	721	0324
Chestnut	301	0349
Honey	436	0373
Dark blue	311	0150

STITCHING INSTRUCTIONS

● Cut a piece of Aida fabric not less than 18 x 22cm [7 x 8¾ inches] and hem the raw edges [see page 4].

● Remember, all the projects in this book were stitched on 11-count Aida. This means that there are 11 stitches to 2.5cm [1 inch].

● Mark the position of the centre stitch [see page 5].

● Thread your needle with three strands of green stranded cotton (floss) and look at the chart on page 7. You will see that the central stitch has been marked. Work this stitch in green

and continue to work across and down towards the basket, keeping the top stitch facing in the same direction [see picture on page 5].

● You can choose which colour to stitch next, the yellow or the blue. To make the work easier to handle you can turn it upside down and work towards the top of the balloon, but remember to turn the chart the same way.

● Continue working all the cross stitches in the same way, finishing off the ends as you go [see page 5]. Remove the threads marking the centre. Check for missed stitches and then add the outline.

OUTLINING

● Thread your needle with two strands of dark blue stranded cotton (floss). Add the outline in back stitch following the chart, and working around the blocks of colour as shown.

● You can work the outline on the basket and the ropes in blue as on the chart, or in the chestnut shade as seen in the colour picture on page 9.

● The hot-air balloon is part of the alphabet sampler at the beginning and end of the book and in the picture on pages 16 and 17.

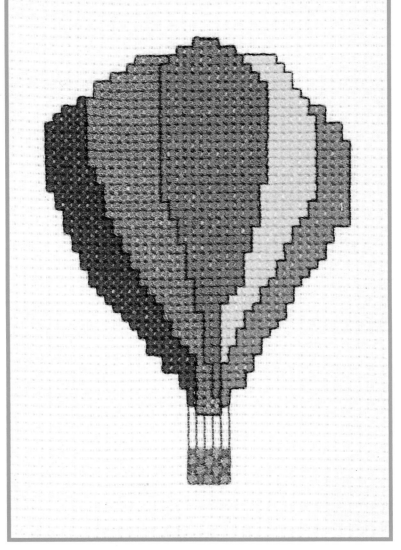

MOUNTAIN BIKE

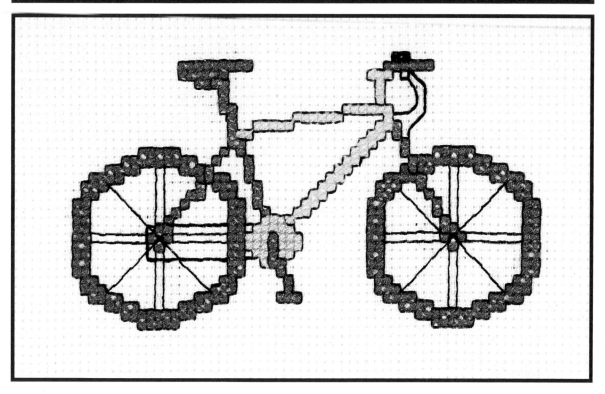

CHART KEY

COLOUR	DMC	ANCHOR
Pink	602	063
Yellow	743	0298
Blue	797	0133
Grey	415	0398
Black	Noir	0403

● All the dimensions are given for Aida fabric, 11 stitches to 2.5cm [1 inch].

STITCHING INSTRUCTIONS

● Cut a piece of Aida fabric 23 x 17cm [9 x 6½ inches] and hem the raw edge. Mark the position of the centre stitch (see page 5).

● Thread your needle with three strands of yellow stranded cotton (floss). Look at the chart opposite and count the squares from the middle empty square to the first yellow cross.

● Begin stitching the pattern here, working down towards the grey section. Check pages 4 and 8 if you want to remind yourself how to start.

● Finish off the threads as shown on page 4 and 5 before starting another colour.

● Work all the cross stitches following the chart, using three strands of stranded cotton (floss) for all of the colours. Remove the threads marking the centre.

OUTLINING

● When the cross stitch has been completed and you have checked that you have not missed any stitches, add the outlining. This is all done in back stitch [see page 4].

● Thread your needle with two strands of black stranded cotton (floss). Following the chart, work back stitch around the cross stitch on the wheels, pedals and handlebars. When this is finished, add the back stitch lines which make up the spokes in the wheels and the brake cables.

MOUNTAIN BIKE

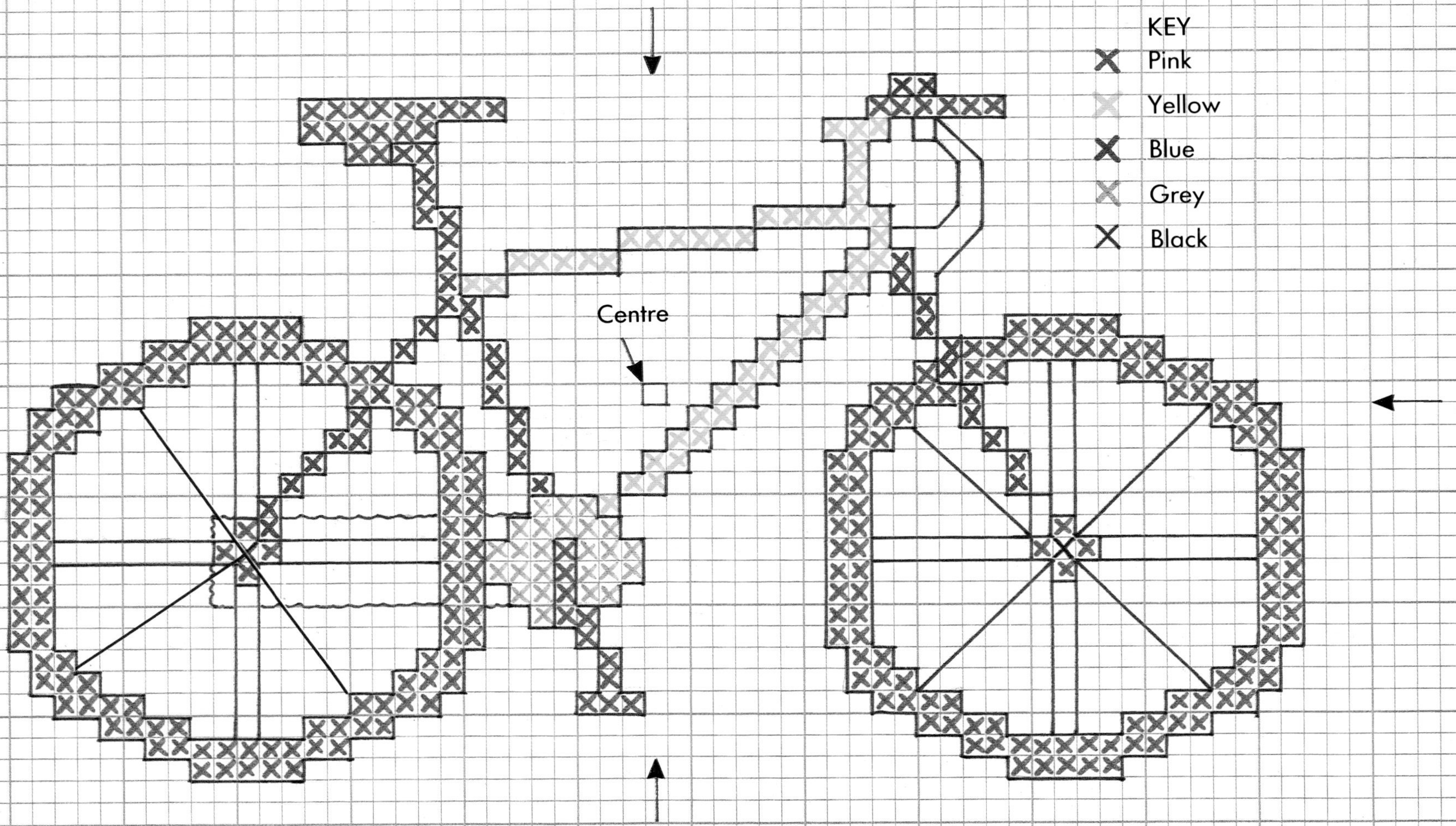

KEY
Pink ✗
Yellow ✗
Blue ✗
Grey ✗
Black ✗

Centre

RACING CAR

CHART KEY

COLOUR	DMC	ANCHOR
Blue	797	0133
Light grey	415	0398
Red	304	047
Black	noir	0403
Dark grey	317	0400
Brown	640	0393
Yellow	743	0298
Flesh pink	754	0881
White	blanc	01

STITCHING INSTRUCTIONS

● If you wish to copy the design in the photograph above, you will find the border chart on page 30. If you are going to include a border, add 5cm [2 inches] to the dimensions below.

● Cut a piece of Aida fabric 23 x 17cm [9 x 6½ inches] and hem the raw edges. Mark the centre of the material as shown on page 5.

● Thread your needle with three strands of yellow stranded cotton (floss). Look at the chart opposite and count down from the central square towards the driver's helmet. Work the helmet and finish off the threads (see page 5).

● Re-thread your needle with red and work the engine cover as shown on the chart. Work all the racing car in three strands of stranded cotton (floss). When you have finished, check for missed stitches and then add the outline.

● For the flag, thread your needle with three strands of black stranded cotton (floss).

● Carefully count up from the car to the bottom corner of the flag and stitch as illustrated.

OUTLINING

● All the outlining on the car and the solid lines under the car are worked in back stitch in two strands of black stranded cotton (floss) – see pages 4–5 for back stitch.

● The words 'Grand Prix' are added in exactly the same way. Count the position of the writing from the driver's helmet.

RACING CAR

Grand Prix

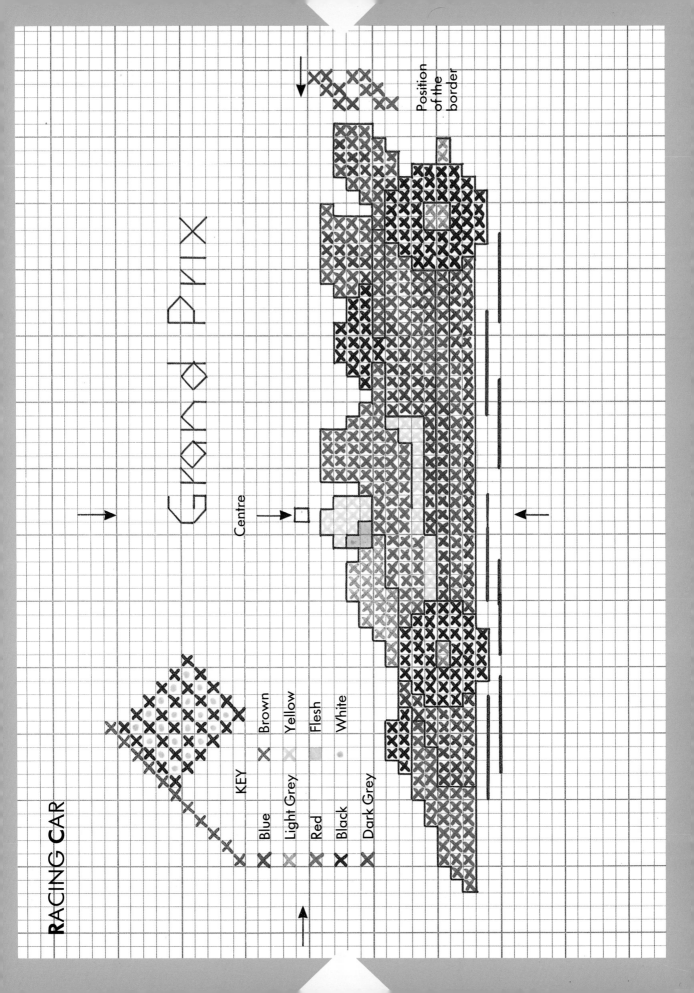

Position of the border

Centre

KEY

✕ Blue	✕ Brown	Yellow
Light Grey	Red	Flesh
✕ Black	· White	
✕ Dark Grey		

SPACE SHUTTLE

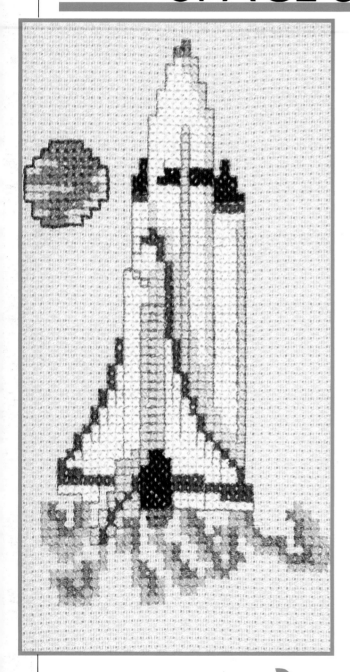

CHART KEY

COLOUR	DMC	ANCHOR
Light grey	415	0398
Black	noir	0403
Royal blue	824	0164
Dark grey	317	0400
Off-white	ecru	0387
Bright pink	891	035
Orange	722	0323

STITCHING INSTRUCTIONS

● Cut a piece of Aida fabric at least 25 x 18cm [9¾ x 7¼ inches] and hem the raw edges. Mark the centre as shown on page 5.

● Thread your needle with three strands of royal blue stranded cotton (floss). Look at the chart opposite and work the blue stitch marked as the centre. Work down the rocket towards the flames.

● When you reach the black section at the bottom of the rocket, finish off the blue thread neatly at the back. Re-thread your needle with black thread and work the black section.

● Thread your needle with light grey and work up toward your starting position. This done, it will be easy to fill in the off-white area on the wings.

● Complete the shuttle, rocket flames and the moon in the same way and check for missed stitches. Remove the threads marking the centre.

OUTLINING

● The outline on the rocket is stitched in back stitch with two strands of dark grey. If you want to make the shuttle stand out more, you could use black or blue for the outlining.

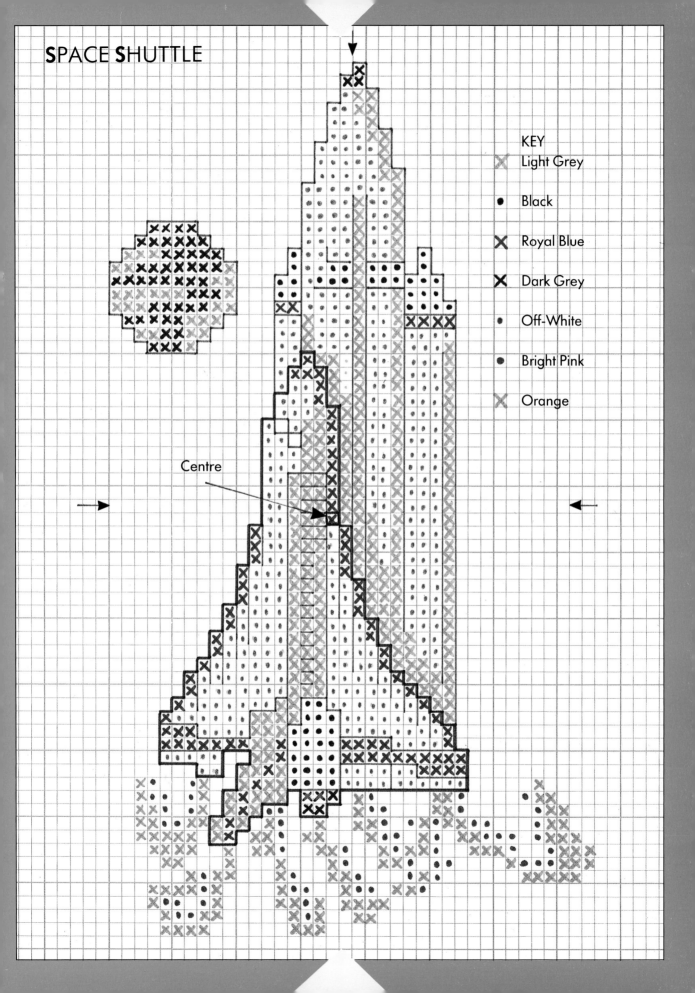

SPACE SHUTTLE

KEY

✕	Light Grey
•	Black
✕	Royal Blue
✕	Dark Grey
•	Off-White
•	Bright Pink
✕	Orange

Centre

SAILING BOAT

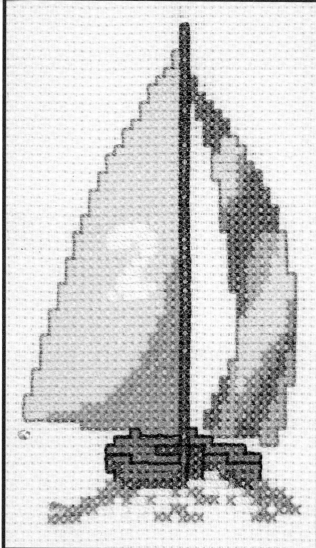

CHART KEY

COLOUR	DMC	ANCHOR
White	blanc	01
Green	562	0216
Pale green	966	0214
Orange	722	0323
Brown	420	0375
Yellow	743	0298
Blue	809	0130
Honey	436	0373
Dark brown	898	0381

STITCHING INSTRUCTIONS

● Cut a piece of Aida fabric at least 23 x 27cm [9 x 10½ inches] and hem the raw edges. Mark the position of the centre stitch as shown on page 5.

● Thread your needle with three strands of yellow. Look at the chart opposite and work the yellow centre stitch.

● Work down and across towards the orange area of the sail. Work as much of the yellow as you want, followed by the orange and brown.

● Try to leave the white number and surf on the water until last, as white tends to become grubby quite quickly!

OUTLINING

● The outlining on this project is worked in three colours. The sails are outlined in blue, the mast in brown and the boat in dark brown. In all cases use two strands of stranded cotton (floss) for the back stitch.

ADAPTING THE DESIGN

● If you have a boat with a number or a letter on the sail, you can adapt this chart very simply. On page 29 there are numbers and letters which match the style of the number "2" shown on the sail. You could substitute the number on your own boat by following the number chart on page 29.

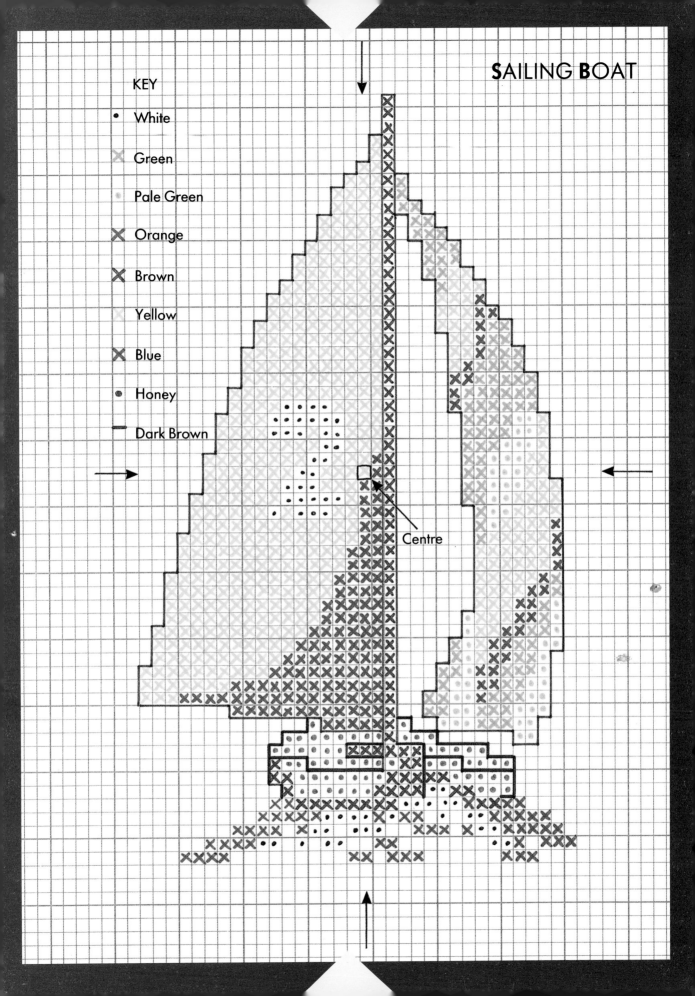

SAILING BOAT

KEY

- • White
- ╳ Green
- ∴ Pale Green
- ╳ Orange
- ╳ Brown
- ╳ Yellow
- ╳ Blue
- • Honey
- — Dark Brown

Centre

PONY AND RIDER

CHART KEY

COLOUR	DMC	ANCHOR
Yellow	743	0298
Pink	891	035
Flesh	754	0881
Honey	738	0372
Dark honey	436	0373
Very dark brown	898	0381
Chestnut	632	0379
Pale honey	951	0366
Grey	414	0399

STITCHING INSTRUCTIONS

● Cut a piece of Aida fabric at least 22 x 21cm [8½ x 8¾ inches] and hem the raw edge. Find the centre and mark as described on page 5.

● Thread your needle with three strands of chestnut stranded cotton (floss) and work the stitch marked as the centre on the chart first. Work towards the rider's pink jacket.
● Complete the cross stitch, following the charts as you stitch. When all the cross stitching is complete, check for missed stitches and then add the outline. Remove the threads marking the centre stitch.

OUTLINING

● All the outline on the pony and rider is worked in two strands of very dark brown.

ADAPTING THE CHART

● The rider in the chart has long hair. If you want to alter the chart to give the rider short hair, it is very simple to do. Or you can change the hair colour if you wish.

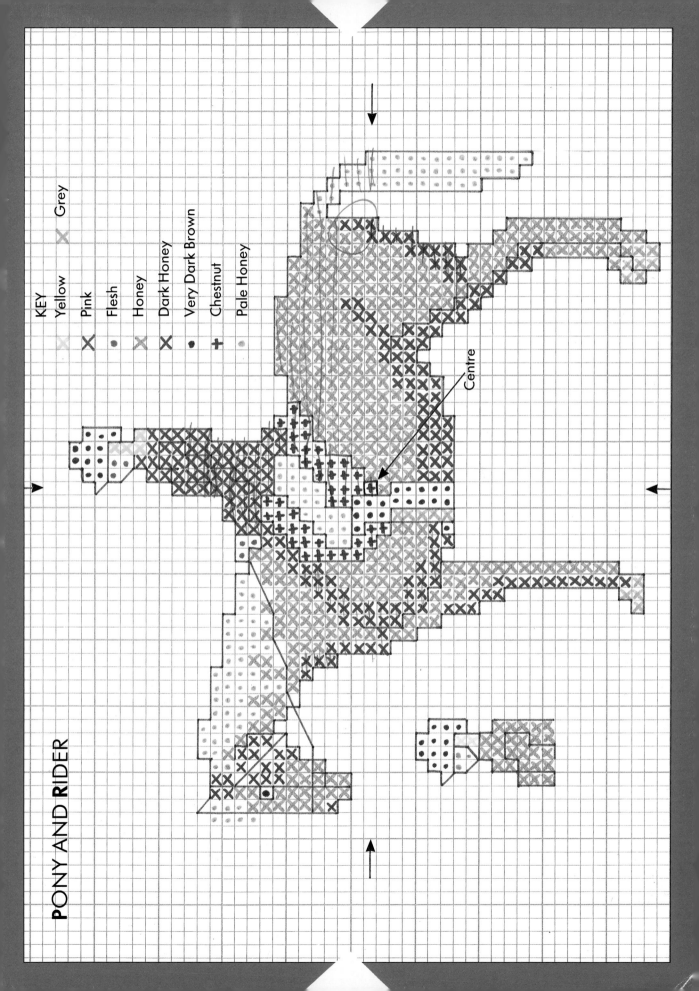

PONY AND RIDER

KEY
Yellow
Pink
Flesh
Honey
Dark Honey
Very Dark Brown
Chestnut
Pale Honey
Grey

Centre

MOTORBIKE

CHART KEY

COLOUR	DMC	ANCHOR
Light grey	415	0398
Dark grey	317	0400
Bright pink	350	011
Black	noir	0403
Honey	738	0372
Yellow	722	0323

STITCHING INSTRUCTIONS

● Cut a piece of Aida fabric 20 x 16cm [8 x 6½ inches] and hem the raw edges. Find the centre of the material and mark as described on page 5.

● Thread your needle with three strands of black stranded cotton (floss). Using the chart, work the rectangular section just below the pink fuel tank.

● Re-thread your needle with three strands of pink thread and work all the top section following the chart.

● Stitch all the cross stitch and check for missed stitches.

● Remove the threads marking the centre stitch.

OUTLINING

● The back stitch outline is worked in two colours, the grey engine areas in black and the pink sections in dark grey.

● All outlining is stitched using two strands of stranded cotton (floss).

● After outlining the cross stitch, add the spokes in the wheels in black.

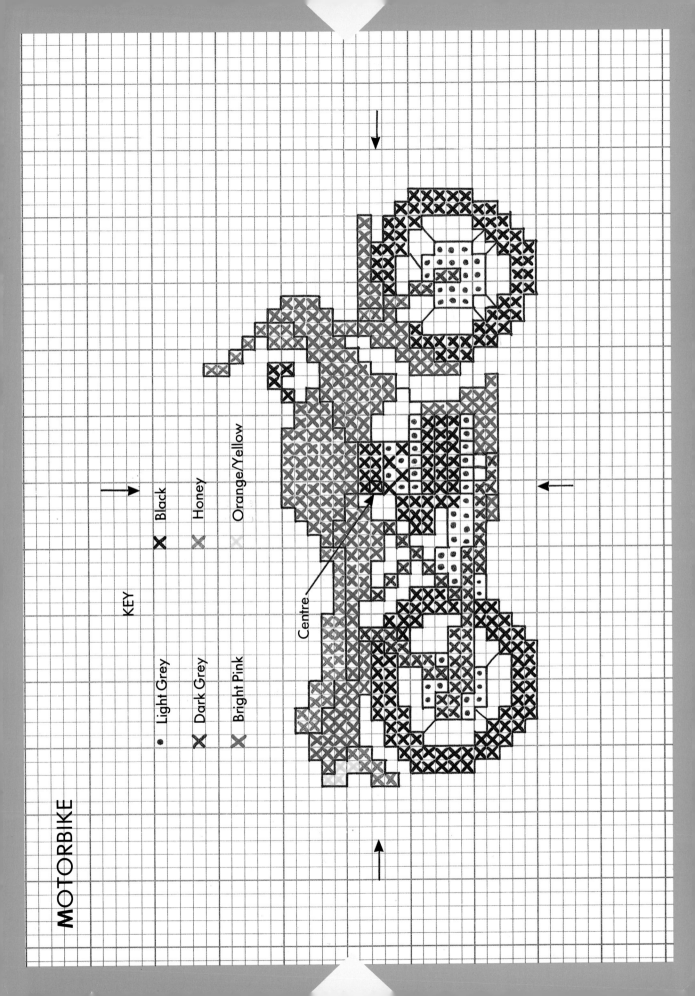

MOTORBIKE

KEY

	Light Grey	✕	Black
✕	Dark Grey	✕	Honey
✕	Bright Pink	✕	Orange/Yellow

Centre

designing your own picture

The beauty of cross stitch is that you can alter the designs to suit your own colour scheme. As you can see from the picture above, the single shoe has been worked from the chart, but in many different colours. You could add a pair of brightly coloured sports shoes to the alphabet to make a new design. In the picture above a sports shoe has been added to my daughter's name as a name plate for her bedroom door.

The charts that follow include the shoe, the alphabets and the small hot-air balloons. The small balloons can be seen at the beginning and the end of the book as part of the sampler design. The small balloons opposite were added to the large design on page 9 and the alphabet from the next four charts.

If you want to use parts of these charts to make your own designs, copy what you need on squared graph paper. Cut them out and move them around until you are satisfied with the shape. Then glue them to a sheet of paper and stitch your own masterpiece!

HAPPY DESIGNING!

HOT-AIR BALLOONS AND SPORTS SHOE

KEY

⊠ Light Grey

⊠ Dark Grey

⊠ Bright Blue

⊠ Green

⊠ Red

⊠ Bright Pink

⊠ Yellow

• Light Blue

⊠ Brown

White

ALPHABETS

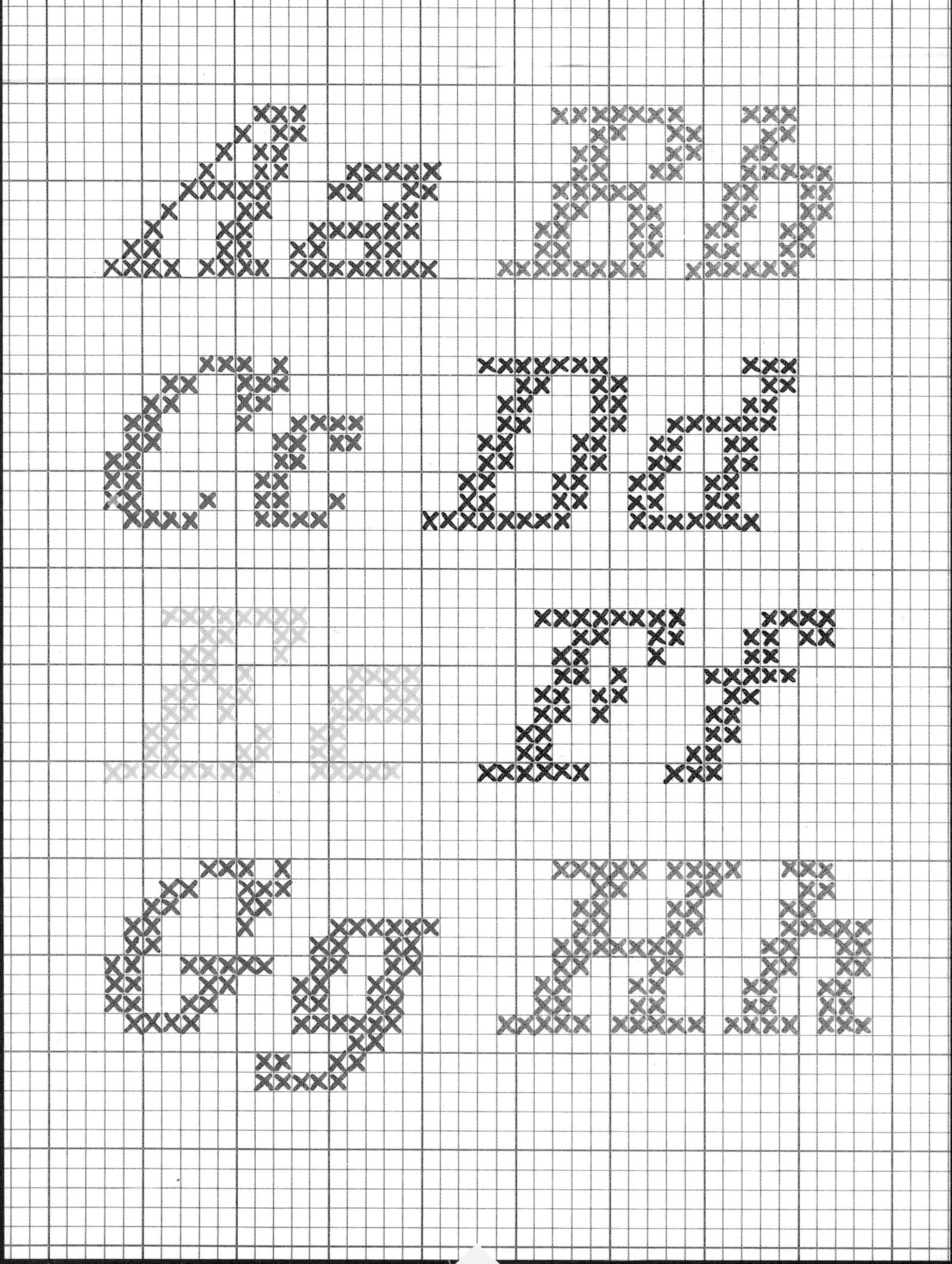

ALPHABETS

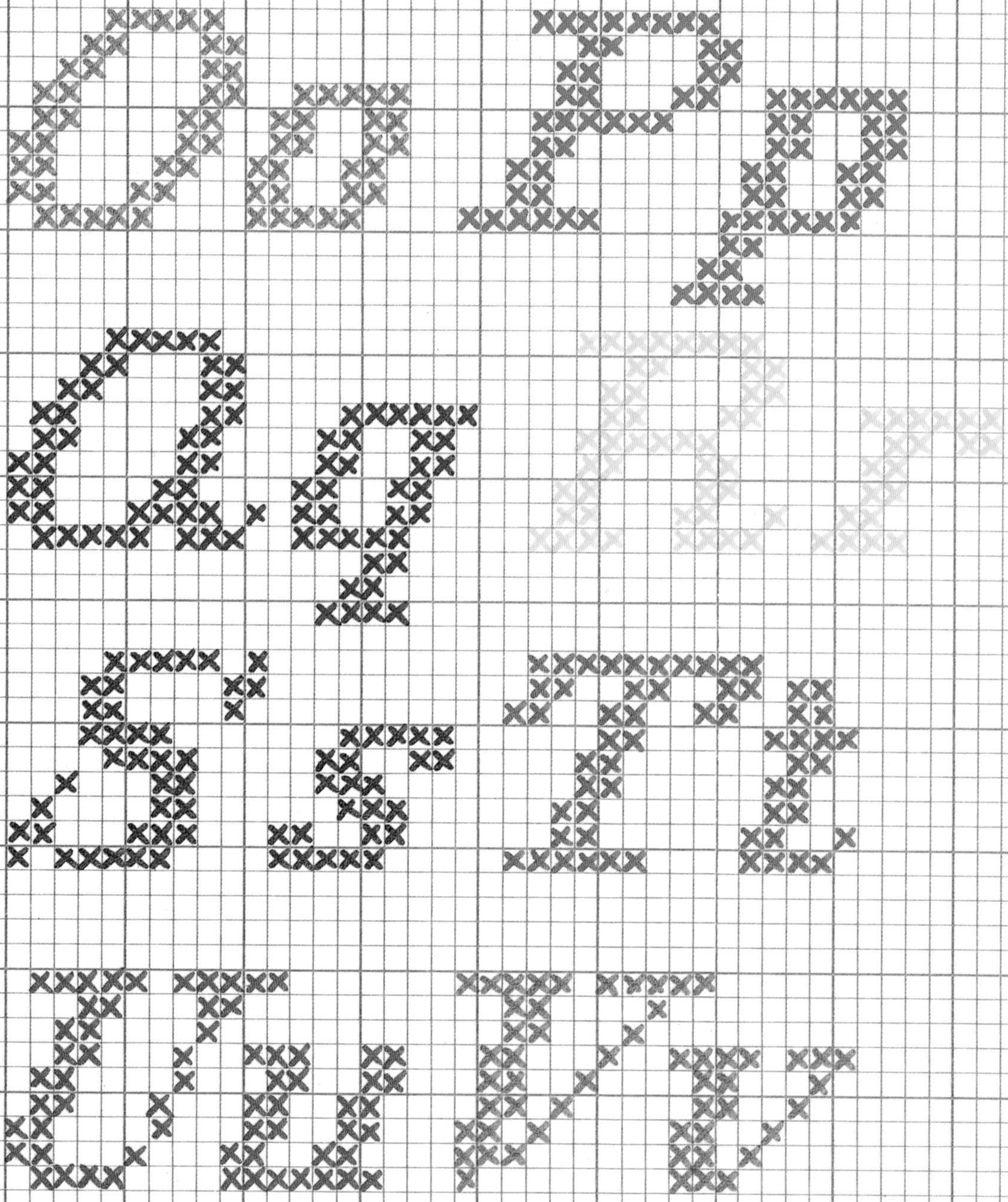

ALPHABETS AND NUMBERS

KEY

✗ Grey		✗ Yellow		✗ Green
✗ Orange		✗ Red		
✗ Blue		✗ Pink		

SIMPLE BORDERS

washing and ironing cross stitch

Here are a few simple tips to follow when you have finished a piece of cross stitch and wonder what to do next.

WASHING

Try to avoid washing your piece at all. Keep your stitching in a safe clean place, away from pets and worst of all, food and drink.

Even in the best-run homes accidents will happen, so it may be necessary to wash a piece of stitching. If you have used either of the brands of thread mentioned in the book, there is no danger of the colour running as long as you wash the item in warm water by hand. Allow the material to dry naturally and then press as below [do NOT use the tumble dryer].

IRONING

Before using a hot iron, check with an adult. Ask for help rather than burning your work or worse still yourself!

Heat the iron to a hot setting and use the steam button if your iron has one. Cover the ironing board with a THICK layer of towelling. I use four layers of bath towel.

Place the stitching on the towel, right side down, with the back of the work facing you. Press down on the piece firmly.

Cross stitch can be made into cards, pictures and books. You can experiment with your projects as you become more experienced. There are dozens of excellent books showing making up and finishing techniques.

HAPPY STITCHING!

acknowledgements

I would like to thank all the people who have made this book possible. My husband Bill, who continues to support my efforts when most would have moved out! James and Louise, my children who gave me the idea, and Vivienne Wells at David & Charles who believed in it!
Michel Standley and all the Inglestone Team who keep things running smoothly in my absence. Simon Apps for photography.
A special thank-you to the Head Teacher, Jon Allnutt, and to Beryl Booker at Fairford School, Gloucestershire, for all their help, particularly for lending me my team of advisers and stitchers without whom this book would not have happened!
My school advisers and stitchers were James Ktoris, Toby Brown, Michael Bowman, Sarah Grundy, Emily Whitehead, Sarah Compton, Steven Watson, Nicola Whiteman, Alison Martin, Natalie Doble, Charlotte Joyner, Lindsay Compton, Laura Hubbard-Miles, Lucy Scrivens, Jonathan Easey, Jennifer Easey, Rebecca Goozee, Jonathan Rishton and Kelly Benfield.
My faithful team of stitchers who stitch and check patterns, including Vera Greenoff, Tamsin O'Brien, Dorothy Presley, Carol Lebez and Hanne Castelo.
Cara Ackerman of DMC Creative World for the generous supply of fabrics and threads, and Tunley and Son for all art and framing supplies.

index

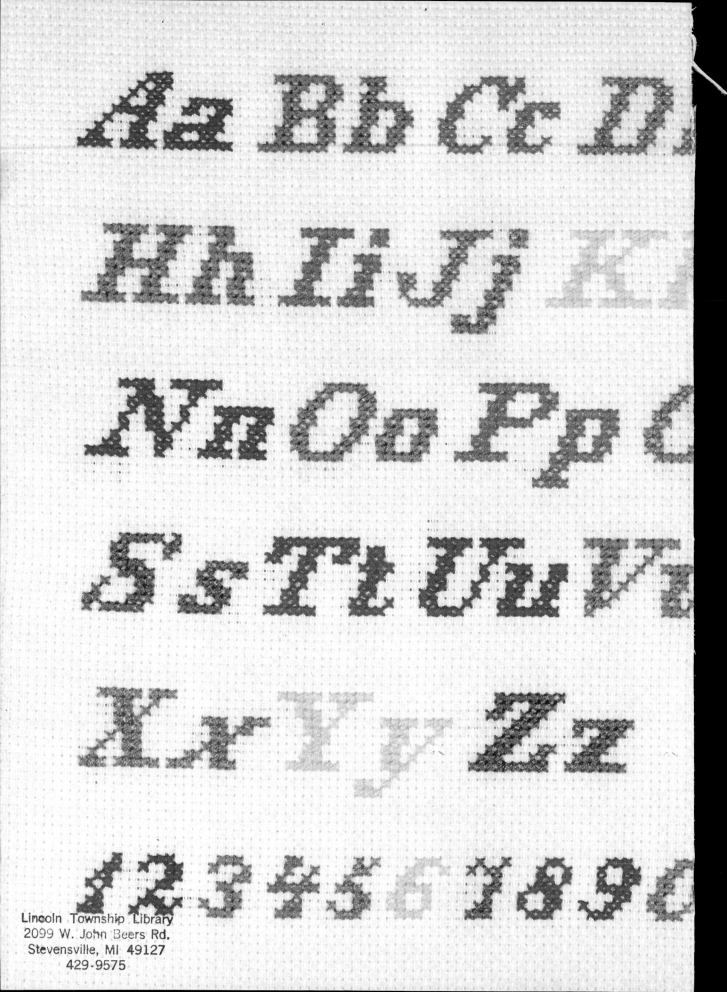

FOOD AROUND THE WORLD

Food in the Caribbean

Polly Goodman

PowerKiDS
press.

New York

Published in 2008 by The Rosen Publishing Group, Inc.
29 East 21st Street, New York, NY 10010

Copyright © 2008 Wayland/The Rosen Publishing Group, Inc.

First Edition

Editor: Sarah Gay
Senior Design Manager: Rosamund Saunders
Designer: Tim Mayer
Consultant: Susannah Blake

Library of Congress Cataloging-in-Publication Data

Goodman, Polly.
  Food in the Caribbean / Polly Goodman. — 1st ed.
     p. cm. — (Food around the world)
  Includes index.
  ISBN-13: 978-1-4042-4299-9 (library binding)
  1. Cookery, Caribbean—Juvenile literature. 2. Food habits—Caribbean Area—Juvenile literature. I. Title.
  TX716.A1G66 2008
  641.59729—dc22
                                        2007032648

Manufactured in China

Cover photograph: a colorful street market in Grenada.

Photo credits: Lonely Planet/Michael Lawrence 6, Steve Winter/Getty Images 8, Wayland Picture Library 9, Simon Reddy/Alamy 10, Robert Harding Picture Library Ltd/Alamy 11, Greg Johnston/Danita Delimont 12 , 17, 22 and title page, M. Timothy O'Keefe/Alamy 13, Lonely Planet/Jerry Alexander 14, 18, 19, 20 and 21, Paul Thomas/Danita Delimont 15, Richard Bradbury/Getty Images 16 and cover, eStock/Pictures Colour Library 23, Andrew Sydenham/Anthony Blake Photo Library 24, Franz-Marc Frei/CORBIS 25, Lew Robertson/Jupiter Images 26.

Contents

Words in **bold** can be found in the glossary on page 28

Welcome to the Caribbean

The Caribbean is made up of thousands of islands in the Caribbean Sea. It includes countries such as Cuba, Jamaica, and Puerto Rico.

▼ Over the last 500 years, people from many different countries have settled in the Caribbean.

People from all over the world have brought their own traditions and cooking styles to the Caribbean. Today, Caribbean food is a delicious mixture of many different flavors.

NORTH
AMERICA

N
W   E
S

ATLANTIC
OCEAN

BAHAMAS

TURKS AND CAICOS
ISLANDS

VIRGIN ISLANDS

Barbuda

Antigua

CUBA

PUERTO
RICO

St. Kitts
and Nevis

Montserrat

Guadeloupe

DOMINICAN
REPUBLIC

Domínica

HAITI

Martinique

CAYMAN
ISLANDS

St. Lucia

Barbados

JAMAICA

St. Vincent

Caribbean Sea

Grenada

Tobago

Netherlands
Antilles

Trinidad

CENTRAL

AMERICA

SOUTH

AMERICA

▲ *The Caribbean islands are marked in orange. They stretch across 2,480 miles (4,000 km) off the coasts of North and South America.*

Farming and weather

The Caribbean has a tropical climate, which means it is hot all year round. From June to November, there is a rainy season. Plants need rain and sunshine to grow, so food crops grow well there.

▼ *Many different vegetables grow on this vegetable farm in Cuba.*

Food fact
Most people in the Caribbean grow fruit and vegetables in their own gardens.

◀ Every banana tree grows a single bunch of from 50 to 150 bananas.

Many crops, such as sugar cane, rice, bananas, coffee, and spices, are grown on big farms called **plantations**. Most of the crops grown on plantations are sold at supermarkets in countries all over the world.

Rice, bread, and spices

Rice is served at almost every Caribbean meal. In Cuba, yellow rice is made with saffron, a yellow spice. Many different types of bread are also eaten. **Roti** and **dhalpourri** are Indian flatbreads that are popular in Trinidad.

◀ The Jamaican dish, rice and peas, is made with coconut, milk, and spices.

Spices are very important in Caribbean cooking. Nutmeg is the most common spice in Grenada, and pimento is popular in Jamaica. Chili peppers are used to make hot pepper sauces on the island of Puerto Rico.

▲ *Spices add flavor and color to Caribbean food.*

Food fact

Before people had fridges, spices covered the taste of meat that had turned bad in the heat.

Fruit and vegetables

The Caribbean is famous for its exotic fruits, such as pineapples, **ackee**, and **guava**. Coconut is used in breads, cakes, ice cream, drinks, and sauces. **Plantains** look a little like bananas, but they are cooked before they are eaten.

◀ *These women in Grenada are carrying trays of mangoes and* **breadfruit** *to sell to tourists.*

Vegetables are the main foods of the Caribbean and are made into stews, soups, and curries. **Yams** are baked, fried, or boiled like potatoes. **Cassava** can be ground and made into flour.

▲ *In Honduras, bread made from cassava flour is baked over a fire.*

Food fact

Coconut water, carrot punch, **soursop** juice, and banana milkshakes are popular Caribbean drinks.

Fish and meat

On the Caribbean coast, people eat fresh seafood, such as crab, **conch**, and shark. Fish can be barbecued, stewed, or curried. Fish used to be **preserved** in salt, and salted fish is still part of many Caribbean dishes, such as ackee and saltfish.

▼ Ackee and saltfish is eaten for breakfast in Jamaica.

Chicken, goat, and pork are popular types of meat. They are usually cooked in stews or curries. Meat is often eaten "**jerk**" style, that is, coated in a spicy mixture and slowly cooked in a pit or barbecued.

◀ This man sells conch shells in Grenada.

Food fact

Pickled pigs' trotters are a popular dish in Trinidad.

Shopping and street food

Every town in the Caribbean has a busy market, where fresh fruit, vegetables, fish, chickens, and eggs are sold. Every village and town has a bakery that sells bread and a general store that sells household goods.

▼ This busy street market is selling all kinds of fruit and vegetables.

Street food is very popular in the Caribbean. Most busy streets have mobile stalls selling ice cream, banana chips, or freshly roasted peanuts. Other stalls serve roasted corn, barbecued chicken, hot peppered shrimp, and fried fish.

▲ An oil drum has been made into a barbecue to cook jerk chicken at this stall.

Mealtimes in the Caribbean

Everyday Caribbean meals might include dishes from the menus below.

Breakfast

Corn porridge
Ackee and saltfish
Banana bread
Tropical fruit salad
Cereal

Coffee
Fresh pineapple juice

Lunch

Grilled jerk chicken
Five-spice roast chicken
Grilled, **marinated** fish

Coffee flan

Ginger ale
Fresh watermelon juice

▶ A dish of jerk chicken, ackee and saltfish, goat meat, and fried plantains.

▲ *A Cuban family eat a meal together.*

Dinner

Callaloo soup
Pick-up saltfish (dried, salted cod and
chili with a lime dressing)
Deep-fried saltfish in batter with a hot
pepper sauce

Tomato and coconut fish stew
Curried goat with rice

Rum and chocolate pudding
Coconut ice cream

Coffee

Around the islands

Caribbean food is a mixture of cooking styles from all over the world. Cuban cooking uses a mixture of Spanish, African, and Mexican foods. Jamaica, Barbados, and Grenada have more African dishes.

▼ **Tamales** is a Mexican dish that is popular in Cuba.

Martinique, Haiti, and St. Lucia were once controlled by the French, so there are many French dishes. Trinidad has the largest number of Asian **immigrants**, so curries and other Indian dishes are popular.

▲ Gumbo, an African soup, is prepared on a Jamaican beach.

Special occasions

Every Saturday, it is traditional to make a big soup for lunch using leftover vegetables from the week. On Sundays, most families share a big lunch of roast chicken or a curry.

◀ This street vendor is serving a plate of fried dough balls with pineapple at a fishing festival in St. Lucia.

◄ These girls are wearing traditional costumes for a carnival parade in Guadeloupe. Most islands celebrate carnival in February each year.

The biggest celebration of the year on each Caribbean island is carnival. It is celebrated on most islands with street parades and roadside food stalls. Fried chicken, chilled coconut water, and sweet tamarind balls are sold by street **vendors**.

Festival food

Most people in the Caribbean are Christians. There are also many Hindus and Muslims, and people who follow traditional African religions. Every religious celebration involves eating special food.

◀ *Christian families enjoy a special Christmas pudding together.*

At Christmas, Christians eat whole roast pig, goat, or turkey. At Easter, grilled fish and Easter buns (spicy cakes) are enjoyed.

Phagwa is a festival celebrated by Hindus in the Caribbean. Many Hindus are **vegetarian**, so vegetarian dishes, such as pumpkin, curried potatoes, and eggplant with rice and dahl are eaten.

▲ Hindus in Trinidad spray colored powder on each other at Phagwa.

Make a banana milkshake!

What you need

4 bananas

1 cup (200 ml) vanilla ice cream

½ cup (100 ml) milk

½ teaspoon nutmeg

What to do

1. Peel the bananas and cut them into thick slices.
2. Put all the ingredients into a food processor or blender.
3. Blend the ingredients until smooth.
4. Pour the milkshake into two glasses and serve with straws.

Ask an adult to help you make this milkshake, and always be careful with sharp knives.

A balanced diet

This food pyramid shows which foods you should eat to have a healthy, **balanced diet**.

We shouldn't eat too many fats, oils, cakes, and candies.

Milk, cheese, meat, fish, beans, and eggs help to keep us strong.

We should eat plenty of vegetables and fruit to keep healthy.

Bread, cereal, rice, and pasta should make up most of our diet.

Caribbean meals use all foods from the pyramid. Some Caribbean dishes are fried in oil but most are made from rice, fruit, and vegetables, with some meat, fish, or beans, which helps to balance Caribbean diets.

Glossary

ackee a red and cream fruit that grows on trees

balanced diet a diet that includes a mix of different foods, which supply all the things a body needs to keep healthy

breadfruit a large, round fruit that is usually served as a vegetable

cassava a vegetable that can be ground into flour

conch a shellfish that has sweet, pink meat inside

dhalpourri an Indian bread seasoned with split peas

guava a round fruit with a thin, yellow skin

immigrant someone who moves to a new country to live

marinated soaked in a savory sauce to add flavor

Phagwa a Hindu festival celebrating the triumph of good over evil

pickled food that is kept in vinegar to stop it from rotting

plantain a vegetable that looks like a banana

plantation a large farm where crops are grown to be sold abroad

preserved kept from turning bad

jerk a style of cooking where meat or fish is covered in spices and cooked on a barbecue

roti a type of Indian flatbread

soursop a green fruit with a spiny skin

tamales parcels of meat or beans wrapped in corn pancakes and steamed

vegetarian a person who does not eat meat or fish

vendor a seller

yam a vegetable that can be steamed, boiled, mashed, grilled, roasted, or fried

Further information

Books to read

A World of Recipes: The Caribbean by Julie McCulloch
(Heinemann, 2001)

Foods of the Caribbean (A Taste of Culture) by Barbara Sheen Busby
(KidHaven Press, 2007)

Kids Around the World Celebrate!: The Best Feasts and Festivals from Many Lands by Lynda Jones (Jossey-Bass, 1999)

Let's Eat! What Children Eat Around the World by Beatrice Hollyer
(Henry Holt and Co, 2004)

Letters From Around the World: Jamaica by Ali Brownlie Bojang
(Cherrytree Books, 2006)

Web Sites
Due to the changing nature of Internet links, PowerKids Press has developed an online list of Web sites related to the subject of this book. This site is regularly updated. Please use this link to access this list:
www.powerkidslinks.com/faw/caribbean

Index

All the numbers in **bold** refer to photographs.